High Income Producing Skills

7 Skills And Habits That Will Generate A 6 Figure Income

Passive Income

7 Predictable Ways to Generate a Passive Income Stream when you are over 40 and While Working a Full Time Job

Introduction

I want to thank you and congratulate you for downloading the book, *"High Income Producing Skills: 7 Skills And Habits That Will Generate A 6 Figure Income"*.

This book has actionable information on the 7 skills and habits that you can develop to help you generate a 6 figure income.

They say money cannot buy happiness (which is true) but the truth is, there is something that financial abundance can give you that very few things in the world can. In other words, financial abundance can create a conducive environment for happiness to thrive because happiness cannot just thrive on its own; it needs the right environment for it to develop and thrive.

This explains why we all strive to attain financial independence with the hopes that it will make us happy. Living a comfortable life, free from the worries brought about by financial instability and insecurity is definitely a goal worth keeping. With financial stability comes the freedom to live life the way you want, not having to worry about micromanaging your little available income.

Unfortunately, as you are well aware, financial independence does not come easy. In fact, many are the times when we try multiple times only to fail repeatedly. What's funny however is just how some people are able to attain financial freedom within a short period yet others live until their retirement years without ever attaining financial independence. What makes the difference?

Well, the secret is in building the right habits because as Will Durant put it, "*We are what we repeatedly do. Excellence, then, is not an act, but a habit.*" For you to attain financial independence, you have to build the right financial habits to propel you to the success you want. It starts with building habits that enable you to make more money first! And if you combine the right habits with some skills, you can be sure that you will rocket-fuel yourself to anything you want to become. This book will give you actionable information on 7 skills and habits that you can build to build a 6 figure income. Let's begin.

Thanks again for downloading this book. I hope you enjoy it!

Table of Contents

Book 1

Book 2

Before we discuss the skills and habits that you can build to put you on the path to a 6 figure income, let's start by building an understanding of how having the right skills and habits helps you to earn a 6 figure income.

Chapter 1: How Having the Right Skills and Habits Helps You Earn a 6 Figure Income

If there are 2 people, one who has been a lumberjack all his life and another who was just handed a saw and has never cut a tree his entire life, which of the two do you think will cut a big tree faster? Well, naturally, the first guy would definitely get it done fast mainly because he has the necessary expertise to cut trees.

This principle applies in all other aspects of life i.e. you can only get the most stuff done well if you have the necessary skills to actually do what needs to be done to propel you to the success you are looking for. The above example clearly shows that having the right skill is essential if you want to do a job the right way and fulfill your goal. As such, whatever your objective is, you need to find the right skill you need to build, to achieve it and then work on developing it. If your goal is to earn a 6 figure income, there are certain special skills that can help you fulfill it faster.

Before we get to a point of discussing these skills, let's first discuss why it is critical to have the right skills to excel in life.

Why You Need To Have the Right Skills to Build Wealth and Financial Abundance

As you are well aware, a skill simply refers to the ability to carry out a task really well. You can think of it as expertise in a certain area. When you have a certain skill, you can do a certain task in a better, more effective and efficient manner compared to if you don't have the necessary skill. Why is that so? Well, the truth is; that certain skill helps bring the following changes in you and your productivity.

- When you have a certain skill, you are able to understand certain tasks better. This in turn makes it easier for you to execute such tasks with greater ease, effectiveness and efficiency. As a result, you can be sure of better quality output within a shorter period. Let me use an example of baking a pie; if you have never baked a pie before, you are quite likely to make a terrible pie in the first attempt even if you know the steps that you need to take (e.g. are following a written recipe). Yes, you can improve with practice but who knows the number of attempts it will take you perfect your pie. However, if you take a baking course (online or offline) and do it consistently, you will soon have good baking skills, which will enable you to bake a nice pie easily. Through training, you will become aware of the different baking hacks and tricks that will help you avoid making mistakes while baking. All this will ultimately work together to ensure you have a great pie.

That's not all; when you have the right skill for performing a certain task, you are able to do it in a record time without compromising on quality. Think of driving for instance; if you are still a beginner driver, you will be very mechanical in what you are doing to an extent that you will end up driving unnecessarily slow. That's unlike being an experienced driver; with years of experience in driving, driving comes naturally to you and you don't waste time in making decisions while driving. If I drive the point home to something related to making money; if you are a beginner programmer for instance, you are likely to take hours upon hours in creating a functioning website, software, app, plug in etc. But if you are good at what you do because you have the necessary skills, you won't take too much time getting things done. This essentially means you can complete your clients' requests within a short period so that you can take more work. The same applies to having skills like copyrighting; as a pro, you will undoubtedly take less time to complete a single project compared to someone who is just getting started.

- With increased efficiency and speed comes greater productivity. This also sets ground for the establishment of new skills and scouting of new opportunities. Think about it for a moment; if you are a software developer, you could start by using your skill to land customers who will pay you to develop websites/software for them. With time, you may realize that you will no longer be trading your hours for money and instead opt to create software for doing different tasks, which you monetize through subscriptions for instance. What I mean here is that with the right skill, you can spin it off to your advantage to change with the changing times. For instance, Elon Musk developed his skills for coding at an early age. He even created his first video game at 12 years! He didn't know what he wanted to do at that time, but he knew that he needed to have the right skill to figure out what he aspired to have and then achieved it. As a coder, he spearheaded the formation of PayPal, which revolutionized online payment. Had Musk not worked on building the 'coding' skill, it is quite likely he would have never have been part of the team that founded PayPal and went on to become a billionaire.

From the above explanation, you can see that a skill provides you with the necessary expertise, knowledge and power you need to set yourself up for success in whichever way possible.

For these skills to come to fruition, you need to nurture the right habits to support the whole process of skill development and nurturing if you want to achieve your goals without fail.

The Place Of Habits In Building Your Earnings Potential

As important it is to have the right skill to create the necessary avenues to make money, it is equally important to nurture success yielding habits that can propel you towards the success you aspire to have. Man is a creature of habit so whatever we do, whoever we are and the life we have manifested for ourselves is because of our habits. If you feel miserable about your current life, find difficult in managing the household expenses and are nowhere near the financial independence you desire to have, it is because you don't have the right habits that draw financial success and abundance your way. You are likely to be lazy, procrastinate a lot, think negatively, set no goals for yourself and don't practice things to improve. Obviously, even if you have the necessary skills, if you always procrastinate, think negatively of yourself and have a host of other undesirable habits, you can be sure that you won't go far in life.

That's why if you wish to be successful in life and earn a 6 figure income, and even more than that, you need to work on building these success yielding habits. This book will discuss these habits along with 7 skills that will undoubtedly put you centrally at the path to a 6 figure income.

Let's begin with the first skill: copywriting.

DOWNLOAD YOUR FREE BONUS:

<u>Pursue Your Passion E-book</u>: Go to-
http://bit.ly/PursueYourPassionNow

Chapter 2: Skill #1- Copywriting

With the world increasingly becoming a global village, more than ever, the skill of copywriting has become one of the most sought after skills the world over! Individuals and corporates the world over are looking for great writers who can weave content in a way that resonates with the target audience and triggers the needed response. Forget marketers and advertisers; there are guys behind the scenes that develop/write the copy before it is taken up by marketers. Those are the guys that organizations and individuals looking to have an edge over the competition are looking for. And you could be that person!

This high demand explains why copywriting is one of the highest paid professions. While you may assume a copywriter does not make a decent income, this is only true for one with average writing skills. There are brilliant copywriters who make thousands of dollars each month just based on their copywriting skills.

So what exactly is copywriting and how can it help you earn a 6 figure income? Let's discuss that:

What is Copywriting?

In its simplest terms, copywriting is simply writing advertising and promotional material. I already stated that there is a guy behind every great advert, product description, product review, email, blog post, or other promotional material. If you are a copywriter, you are that guy who creates content for billboards, brochures, emails, websites, catalogs, flyers, any promotional material such as pens, caps and mugs and anything else that can be used to advertise a certain good or service. The text that is written by a copywriter is known as a copy and copywriting is a part of a staggering $2.3 trillion direct-response industry all across the globe.

Unlike editorial writing, copywriting is about encouraging the reader to take the desired action, which is usually to make a purchase of the good or service being promoted/advertised. It can also be to opt-in or become involved in some way with the good being advertised or the company being talked about. For instance, if a certain flyer encourages you to do volunteer work in a shelter home, that is its call to action.

Since a copywriter's job is to persuade the reader to take the desired action and convince him/her to use the said product or service (or take a certain action), he/ she is often known as 'salesman in print.' Just like the typical salesman tries to woo a potential customer so he/she actually makes the purchase, a copywriter does the same with the only difference being that a salesman uses his/her antics directly and face-to-face whereas a copywriter uses his/her written words in the copy to do the same.

Just to clarify: Copywriting is not the same as 'copyright"; the two are entirely different. Copyright refers to having the exclusive legal right to create, reproduce, sell, distribute or publish a certain piece of work such as music, artistic item or a book. A copyright protects that material and ensures it isn't used illegally without the authorization of its rightful owner. Any material with this symbol © is designated as a copyrighted material.

I know you might be wondering; but how the heck will you make six figures writing copy when the competition is so fierce even from oversees copywriters who can write just well but at a fraction of the rates you are going to charge?

Let's discuss that:

Can Copywriting Really Enable You To Make 6 Figure Income?

Yes, copywriting is indeed a skill that can help you make a six-figure income and even millions of dollars and there are scores of copywriters who are currently earning six figures writing sales copies for their clients. However, how much you make with this skill depends entirely on the amount of effort and time you invest into it.

Joshua Boswell is one of the popular copywriters who make six figure incomes from copywriting. His story is unique especially because he grew his copywriting business to more than $100,000 a year in as little as 1 year! Danny Margulies is another copywriter who's known for earning over six figures a year, as a freelance copywriter. Ed Gandia has also done it, after 27 months of working his butt off to build his copywriting skill! Clayton Makepeace is another big name in the industry who writes copies that have made over $1.5 billion!

There are countless other examples of people who have made and are still making six figures by leveraging on their copywriting skills. You too can be one of those who start and build your skill to become a six figure copywriter.

On average, a median copywriter with an average skill makes about $47,838 per year and 80% of all copywriters earn between $35k and $65k annually. However, this number increases as your expertise and experience improves.

I know you might be wondering; so why would anyone pay anybody so much money anyway?

Well, the number one reason why copywriting is a huge industry is because there is always something to sell. There are scores of people and corporations that want to get their word out there and get people to respond favorably to their message in order to ultimately increase leads and ultimately sales and profits. Since a lot of money goes into running an advertising/promotional campaign, it would be foolhardy not to invest in a good copy to ensure the message actually brings about the intended response from the audience. As you well know, promotional/advertising campaigns are expected to bring in millions or even billions of dollars for the respective companies. Unfortunately, these companies (advertisers) cannot achieve that if their copy is wanting. That's where copywriting skills come in. And as different companies plan to rake in millions or even billions of dollars in sales or profits, that's where copywriters make their kill!

For you to get to a point of making six figures, you should consistently be able to write a copy that gets the target audience to take whatever action you want them to take without them feeling coerced. The more persuasive your content is, the more customers it will lure in, the more the product will sell and the more you will succeed in this business. It is as simple as that.

Let me give an example; the restaurant industry in the U.S. alone spends over $5.875 billion on advertising every year. Since copywriting is a huge component of advertising, you can well imagine how much a good copywriter can make. This is just the statistic related to the restaurant industry. The automobile, agriculture, medical, pharmaceutical, education and many other industries spend a huge amount on advertising and copywriting every year too.

Therefore, if you wish to make 6 figures from copywriting, it is time you start paying more attention to building this skill so you can build and enhance your copywriting skills because as you well know, there is lots of money to make! The question is:

What Do You Need to Do to Become a Copywriter?

There are three amazing things about being a copywriter:

- You can make a 6-figure income through it

- You can work from the comfort of your own home

- You don't have to have a college degree or some special qualifications to become a copywriter.

These three make copywriting one of those professions where anybody can start and be great at it! It is unlike many other professions out there, which require years of formal training to actually 'qualify' to offer your services! With copywriting however, you just have to have a unique flare with words to excel at it! Let's take the discussion a little further:

1: Understand the Landscape

There has been an enormous surge in online content over the past decade, which has created an unprecedented demand for excellent copywriters. A well-written sales copy on a company's website not only provides prospective customers with confidence to buy that advertised good or service, it also enables businesses to easily generate organic web traffic from search engines.

Internet marketing is quite diverse and is moving at a dynamic pace. Copywriters who comprehend the latest trends in copywriting, social media and search engine optimization (SEO have an edge over copywriters who aren't aware of these trends. Therefore, if you wish to become a successful copywriter, you must make yourself comfortable with these trends first. Carry an extensive research on the copywriting trends and strategies in this day and age, and go through them time and again. The more you read about it, the better you will grasp the strategies and trends. You could even enroll for an online course (on Udemy for instance) on some of these things to build a strong understanding of the trends. If you wish not to sign up for a course, you can buy a book on Amazon, watch YouTube tutorials on the same and follow blogs on these trends to ensure you are not left behind. The truth is; it may take some time to settle in, but if you are consistent, you will soon understand the landscape well.

2: Figure Out Your Type

There are many types of copywriters nowadays. As such, it is only fair that if you want to become a successful copywriter, you have to figure out the type you would like to be. There are copywriters who deal primarily in SEO, those who deal in print advertising media only, those that produce content of all sorts and those who are focused on web editing mainly. There are many other types of copywriters; the above are just a few of the many.

You need to find out the type you would like to be in order to gather enough information about it, develop the necessary skills and venture successfully into it. If you are just venturing into copywriting, it would be wise to begin with content writing. This involves writing all sorts of materials from website content to e-books to magazine articles to promotional content. However, if you find it difficult to produce good quality content of all sorts, it is best to pick a type and stick to it. Find out more about the types of copywriting here.

Once you have selected a type, find some renowned copywriters in that category and research on them. Try to get in touch with them if possible and request for their mentorship;

there is nothing as beneficial as having a mentor in the industry you want to succeed in. Therefore, find a mentor if you can and then get guidance from him/ her to succeed in your respective field. A mentor has already achieved things you are aspiring to have and can give you valuable guidance to become successful. If you cannot find a mentor, you may perhaps want to enroll in a copywriting course like this one. You can also find other courses here. On these platforms, you will find lots of valuable information that will hold you by the hand until you succeed.

3: Find the Particular Industry You Would Like to Venture in and Reach Out to People

Successful copywriters pick a particular industry they would like to venture in and familiarize themselves with the jargon, technicalities and trends related to it. This enables them to write amazing copies that 'don't sound off'. Think about writing copy for a tech company dealing with SaaS solutions; you are unlikely to write a good copy if you don't understand the industry well so that you can carefully use words in a manner that gets customers wanting to click the buy, subscribe, bookmark or share button.

Therefore, if you wish to venture into a particular niche, find out which industry you would like to target and become an expert in it. For instance, if you like writing about food, you could target restaurants and hotels and present yourself as a copywriter who writes sales copies related to food and related services. If you feel you are more suited for the telecommunications industry, familiarize yourself with it and then reach out to companies in that industry.

However, this isn't mandatory. You can target as many industries as you like to increase your chances of getting good clients. Whether you decide to stick to one industry or step into many, start reaching out to people.

Luckily, with the advancement in internet, there exists various online forums that can help you get good clients e.g. Upwork, Fiverr, Freelancer, Craiglist and Guru. Create your profile on as many platforms as you can and then start sending proposals to the potential clients there. Each platform has its own procedure and rules so familiarize yourself with them first and then start applying for different job offers.

You will most likely be asked to submit a sample or two to showcase your skills to prospective customers so make sure to create your best copy to provide when needed. If you have any other written sample, attach it even if it is not a sales copy as it showcases your talent and the variation you can bring in your style. Most of the gigs (projects) that you will get from these platforms will be short-term projects. Clients may ask you to do one piece or more for a certain period for them. However, if a client is extremely pleased with your work, he/ she may return for more so make sure to give your best shot in each project.

In addition, check out the different companies you wish to work for on social media forums such as Facebook, LinkedIn and Twitter and get connected with them. Comment on their posts and interact as much as you can on their pages to show your interest in their work. Also, indirectly show your desire to work for/with them and leave them a message about it. However, make sure not to do that repeatedly because you may end up irritating the organization and getting blocked.

Also, get the word out about your new venture into copywriting; you can tell your friends, relatives and just about anyone who cares to give you an audience. Remember that before organizations can pay you to write their sales copy, you will need to attract people with your amazing content. The more you spread the word, the better will be your chances of finding more clients.

4: Create a Compelling Sales Pitch

When you apply for different copywriting projects, ensure to create a compelling sales pitch for each one of them. The people you are aiming to write for need to know why they should choose you and your sales pitch should provide them with all the reasons to pick only you. Discuss your passion for the job, any experience you have in the field, what you can bring to the table, how adept you are in the field, your commitment to your work and other qualities that will impress the prospective client(s).

However, make sure not to oversell yourself. On the reality cooking show 'Kitchen Nightmares', Gordon Ramsay, a renowned American chef always cut backs on the dishes included in the menu because he knows no chef can be an expert in hundreds of dishes. Similarly, you need to accept that you cannot be an expert at marketing, copywriting, social media and SEO at the same time.

As such, never oversell yourself and never write about things you haven't done or those you cannot do well because being dishonest about your skill set may get you a gig or two for now but it will never help you build a good reputation in the industry.

5: Practice and Practice Some More

As you send job proposals to different companies and individuals, don't forget to practice your writing skills. Find different samples of sales copies online and go through them to become more familiar with the work. Next, choose any random product you wish to promote and think of a catchy tagline or a theme you would like to work around.

Brainstorm as many ideas as you can to come with something innovative. When you have something interesting to work with, build up on the idea. Look for good vocabulary that brings out your message clearly and effectively. Remember, copywriters aren't word writers but word choosers. This means that your job won't be to just fill in words even when they don't mean anything, but to come up with some that adds value and substance to the copy so choose your words cautiously.

Your writing must have a clear message and lots of structure in it so go through your final piece a few times to ensure it does not lack substance. Also, be passionately involved in your writing. Think of yourself as that product's/service's customer and then think of what would compel you to make a purchase. Use that insight to come up with compelling content for the sales copy.

Carry out this practice as much as you can. Practice makes a man perfect. While nothing is perfect, things are good enough so practice as much as possible to become better at copywriting. Use your best pieces as samples to get better clients.

You can also consider taking a copywriting course and read as many books as you can on the topic because reading is one powerful way to learn and improve any skill.

6: Be Consistent

Like with everything else, consistency is the key to win. If you want to be a successful copywriter, you need to be consistent in your efforts. You need to practice consistently, reach out to people consistently and send proposals for job offers consistently as well. It may take you some time to land some big clients, but if you are consistent, you will definitely get there. You may have to start small in the start so be prepared to write good content on low rates for a while. On average, new and amateur writers in the U.S get $15 to $30 for a 500 words, but there are many writers who are willing to work for even lower rates. Since you don't have much experience in the field yet, you will have to face fierce competition from these writers so stay strong. If your work is good and you build a good rapport with a client, you will soon start commanding better rates as well.

Consistency is a good habit you will have to nurture to develop the copywriting skill and any other skill as a matter of fact. To build this skill, do the following:

- First, start talking positively to yourself. Often, we find it difficult to do things we are not used to doing or the tough tasks or anything out of the ordinary, because we don't believe in ourselves. If you look closely, you will realize that your negative beliefs about your abilities are deeply rooted in your negative self-talk. Your self-talk refers to the way you talk to yourself (the internal/mental dialogue that you have about different issues in life) and if it is negative, chances are, you will find it difficult to set any meaningful goal for yourself, have an unwavering self-belief and build any skill you want. Hence, start talking nicely to yourself. Each time you say anything disparaging to yourself, 'catch yourself' doing that and change it to something more positive. If you think 'I can never be a six figure copywriter' or 'It is too hard to practice every day', change it to 'If I try, I am sure I'll be a great copywriter who earns 6 figures' or 'Practicing writing is fun if I become involved in it so today, I'll become more engaged in my practice session.' Do this as much as possible and soon, you'll train yourself to engage in positive self-talk only. This will slowly help you nurture a positive mindset which will make it easier for you to become consistent and build important skills.

- Set a certain time of the day to practice your skill. Try to do this task during this time only to cultivate regularity and punctuality. Begin with practicing for 20 minutes and slowly increase the time to 30, 40 and 60 minutes. Do take short breaks after working for 20 minutes so you don't over-exhaust yourself.

- Set nice rewards for yourself that you can indulge in once you are done with the practice session. This reinforces positive behavior and helps you become consistent in building the respective skill.

Practice these steps daily and soon, you'll find yourself improving your skill set. The same steps should be used to nurture other skills that will be discussed in this book. Let us move to the next skill- coding that can set you on the path to a six figure income.

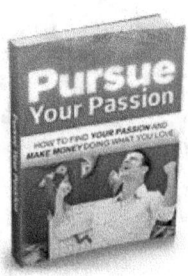

Chapter 3: Skill #2- Coding

Code is the language of the future. In fact, Fastcompany.com considers coding the most important skill of the future. That's for sure, especially given that we are increasingly becoming technology dependent. From the phones we use to the computers we have in our offices to the vehicles, home entertainment systems, to home automation systems to our security systems to our offices, to transportation, telecommunication, aviation, and much more, technology is at the center of the future of humanity. This perhaps explains why coding is regarded as one of the most sought after skill in today's work environment with 8/25 of the top 25 jobs on Glassdoor being tech positions. And it is not just in the technology sector, there is an increasing number of businesses and individuals relying on computer code. Job positions that require coding as a skill also command higher wages. And the good thing is that with this skill, you are just not going to work in the tech industry; coding is now needed in literally every area of the economy including health care, finance, banking, education and even art.

But what exactly does this skill entail? Let's discuss that.

Understanding Coding

Coding is the skill that helps us create applications, websites and software. Your operating system, browser, gaming console, home automation system, apps on your mobile phone, the website/device you are using now and all the social media forums you are a member are all made using coding skills.

A code is simply a language that a computer can understand. Just like humans need a language to communicate with other humans and in their mind, so do computers. But since computers don't use the same language as us humans, we have to input a message that they can understand in order for them to execute different functions. Machines/computers can only understand other machines/computers. And without the necessary mechanism of transferring what's being communicated by computers, humans cannot 'decode' the message. I want you to think of code as a way of translating between 2 normal languages. For instance, think of Chinese and English for instance; there is no way someone who has never learned Chinese can understand it if they are English speakers and vice versa. Therefore, if a Chinese man and English man need to know what the other wants, they have to involve a translator/interpreter. The work of the interpreter in this case would be to pick the message in one language, understand it well then pass the same message to the other side, of course in a different language. Your work as a coder would be to make computers to do whatever it is that you want to do. Computers understand in zeros and ones. Computers can understand only two types of data: one and off since it is a collection of many on and off switches known as transistors. Everything computers do is nothing more than a special combination of certain transistors turned off and some left on.

These combinations are represented as 1s and 0s which is known as the binary code. Every digit in the code symbolizes one transistor. The binary code is then grouped into bytes, which are group of 8 digits, each digit representing one transistor so there are 8 transistors in total. The modern computers today comprises of millions of transistors. Since writing a computer program by simply typing out millions of 0s and 1s is difficult for us, we use code to create a language that computers can understand. There are different programming languages designed to write the binary codes. A coding or programming language is a set of rules that define the right way to write and format a computer code. There are scores of programming/coding languages that help us craft many different websites, application and computer software. These languages allow us to write a code faster without having to write the binary code since the languages translate the input to a binary code.

Now that you have a good understanding of what coding is, let us take a look into its importance.

Why You Need to Build this Skill

A report from Burning Glass, a renowned firm that specializes in creating job market analytics shows that in 2015, there were around 7 million job openings in the country that demanded applicants to have coding skills. The report also shows that programming related jobs are growing at a 12% rate as compared to other skills in the market. Moreover, coding skills are needed in different job categories such as data analysts, scientists, engineers, information technology (IT) worker, designers and artists. It also found out that programming languages such as HTML, JavaScript, Python and C++ were quite in demand.

The report collected data from around 26 million online job postings in the U.S. All its findings prove that coding is indeed a core skill that help bolster your chances of earning a high salary. There are many coding related jobs that pay around $22,000 or more per year and around 49% of coding related jobs pay over $58,000 annually. That's not all; there are many coders who are earning 6 figures easily by creating different applications, websites and software.

According to BLS, coding related jobs will grow by 18.8% until 2024 which shows that coding will definitely be a sought after skill years from now so if you start working on it now, you will be quite adept it in the future.

Moreover, coding is a skill that can bring some other benefits some that can help you directly in making six-figure income. If you know how to code, you can easily design a website for yourself or for the business that you are running; you can create applications for laptops and smartphones; and you can even create new software.

Now that you are better aware of the importance of learning this skill, let us take a look at how you can learn it.

How to Learn Coding

There is no right or wrong method to learn coding, but here are a few good places to start with for beginners.

1: Pick a Language You Want to Learn

There are many programming languages and while it is good to learn as many as possible because each of them has its own pros, you cannot learn all in the start. Hence, pick one that you would like to start with based on what you plan to do. For instance, if you wish to write an iOS app, begin learning Swift. If you want to learn an advanced level language, opt for Python, as it is the most sought after programming language. You can check the comparison of some popular coding languages here.

Before you pick a language, do think about what you wish to do so you can start off with something that helps fulfill your current objective.

2: Start Small and Understand the Basics

A good place to start learning coding is to start small and grasp the basics first. David Sinsky is a self-taught popular coder who learned to code in just 8 weeks. He began with getting an introduction of Python and spent a weekend understanding it only before moving forward. He advises all the people trying to learn coding to do the same- always start small with the basics, break the tasks into smaller steps and then gradually move forward.

3: Use Training Sites, Take Courses, Read Books

There are lots of free online training websites such as Codeacdemy, KhanAcademy and Code.org that provide free tutorials that can help you learn coding. There are also paid courses too that can help you learn coding easily. Research on them online and you'll find lots of courses to suit your needs. Before opting for one, do check reviews and only choose those with good reviews.

Additionally, read books on the subject to help you build sufficient understanding of different concepts on the subject. For instance, there is an enormous collection of around 500 free programming books on GitHub and you can also check out this collection of e-books on 24 coding languages.

4: Use a Kid's App

There are some fantastic coding apps for kids nowadays too. They are simple to understand and use, and are even suitable for all ages. Scratch is one good example of a coding app for kids that is suitable for adults too. Use it when starting out to practice what you learn and as you progress, you can move on to creating your own apps.

5: Practice What You Learn and Play Coding Games

The value of practice cannot be overemphasized. And what better way to practice than to play games; you learn while having fun, right? A good way to make practice sessions fun is to play coding games such as CodinGame and Code Combat.

Focus on these steps and practice them consistently to learn this skill. To ensure you learn it effectively and make the right use of it, break the habit of procrastination. Here is how you can do that.

Building the Habit of Taking Action on Time

To become successful in whatever you do, you need to overcome your urge to procrastinate and start taking action on time. Here is how you can do that.

- First, analyze the harmful effects of procrastination on your life and see how it is keeping you from living your dream life. This will encourage you to break it for good.

- Create your daily to-do list the night before to ensure you are prepared for the next day beforehand.

- Check the first task on the list in the morning and do it without overthinking it. Whatever it is you are supposed to do, just take the first step and if that seems difficult, try the 5 minute hack. Set a timer for 5 minutes and commit to work on a task for only 5 minutes and keep doing that until you complete 20 to 30% of that job. Practice this consistently and soon, you'll nurture the habit to do stuff on time.

- Also, do a task the minute you assign it to yourself so you don't postpone it.

- Reward yourself when you do take action and perform a task on time to reinforce this positive behavior.

Tip: Talk nicely to yourself especially when you have a slip-up and you will soon be able to effectively overcome procrastination when the urge to postpone tasks comes knocking.

With another important skill covered, let us move to the 3rd skill that can help you earn in 6 figures- online marketing.

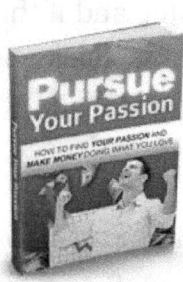

Chapter 4: Skill #3- Online Marketing

The internet has made the concept of global village a reality. With over 3 billion people now having access to the internet, the huge market created by the internet is something that businesses the world over have to find innovative ways to take advantage of. That's where the internet/online marketing skill is increasingly demanded.

What is Online Marketing?

Online marketing is simply a set of tools and methods that are used for promoting products and services through the internet. It (Online marketing) involves identifying the right type of online marketing mix that will appeal to your respective target market and will help turn potential customers into actual customers. A lot of analysis and research goes into selecting the marketing mix as well as measuring how successful each strategy proves to be. There are different methods/approaches of online marketing some of which include the following:

- Search Engine Marketing: This encompasses search engine marketing (SEM) and SEO (search engine optimization). SEO helps improve the ranking of your business website in the search engine listing in a bid to increase organic traffic to your website and improves the chances of sales. SEM is the paid search marketing. You pay a certain fee to search engines and they display your advertisement on the user's search results whenever he/ she searches using any of your keywords. SEM statistics help provide good feedback on your ad's effectiveness.

- Mobile Marketing: Mobile marketing refers to advertising services and goods to people who are using mobile devices like smartphones and tablets. With advancement in technology, you can target people who are using mobile devices to see certain ads on different platforms. This can greatly improve conversions given that a huge part of the access to the internet these days is from mobile devices. Mobile marketing also involves push notifications, SMS marketing etc.

- Email Marketing: When you build a mailing list of people who are likely to want to buy your products or services, you can use email marketing to generate leads and sales. All you will need to do is to send your subscribers emails about your current products/services, keep them up-to-date with the latest promotions and deals, and inform them of any upcoming events. You can even send weekly/monthly newsletters and special offerings to them via email. This keeps your potential customers involved in your business and improves the conversion rate (when a potential customer becomes an actual customer.)

- Online Advertising: There are lots of different types of advertisement options available online such as banner ads, displaying webpages before or after reaching an expected website, text ads and social media ads.

- Social Media Marketing: Social media sites such as Pinterest, Facebook, Twitter, Instagram and LinkedIn are great platforms for marketing goods and services. With these platforms, all you need to do is to create your business account/page and then create interesting posts, videos and other content to draw your target market towards it to increase engagement.

- Blogging: Blogging is a powerful way to promote a business, as it engages the audience, get feedback and much more. You can blog about your product/service, latest trends in the industry or inform them about interesting and upcoming promotions and events to attract them towards your work.

Now that you have a basic understanding of what online marketing entails, let us talk about its importance so you know why you need to work on this skill.

Importance of Online Marketing

1: The market is huge

According to the sales forecasts by eMarketer, e-commerce sales will most probably reach up to $4.058 trillion across the globe by 2020. This whopping figure reflects the ever-increasing trend of online shopping and proves that online marketing is indeed a skill worth building. This presents an opportunity for anyone with great online marketing skills to help those who want to sell online.

Another survey published in 2016 shows that around 54% consumers purchase products online on a monthly or weekly basis. This figure will most likely increase by 2020. This is applicable to most of the industries.

So if the majority of your customers will be making online purchases, it is important to work on building your online marketing skills to ensure you reach out to those who are actually looking for various products and make a sale. You can offer online marketing services to corporates or you can use these skills to market your business, products or services. Since most of your competitors are likely to have an online presence, you too need to jump in the bandwagon then use your online marketing skills to have an edge over the competition, which ultimately enables you to increase your market share.

2: Affordable

You cannot compare the cost of online marketing with offline e.g. print or radio/TV advertising! This is great if you are running a marketing campaign for your business since you won't need to spend a lot of money on advertising. It is also great if you are being hired as an online marketing professional, as you can help your customers to keep marketing costs low while of course ensuring the returns on investment is high.

3: Targeting

The internet provides a wide array of complex tools for performing literally everything. For instance, there are tools for targeting people that meet a certain criteria (e.g. age, gender, geographical location, preferences etc.) so that you can market products/services to them and tools that you can use to measure performance to determine the effectiveness of your marketing campaigns. This ensures you can easily tweak what needs to be tweaked to attain whichever goals you may be having. This is not possible with offline advertising i.e. print, radio and TV. This very feature ultimately ensures that you have more control over your marketing efforts, budget and literally everything about your products/brand.

As you can see, if you run your own business, it is imperative to work towards building this skill. Even if you don't have your own business, you should still consider building this skill because it broadens your horizon and can helps you become an online marketer for other firms. Having online marketing as an added skill commands higher salary in many job positions these days so you shouldn't overlook it.

So how exactly can you develop the skill? Here is how:

How to Learn Online Marketing

Try the following steps and strategies to become a good online marketer.

1: Start Surfing the Web

If you are not much acquainted with the internet, start familiarizing yourself with different online advertising media such as banner ads and online marketplaces like eBay, Amazon and Craiglist.

2: Create Accounts on Different Social Media Platforms

Also, start building a social media presence by creating your accounts on the different social media sites listed above. It is not necessary to have a presence on all of them but targeting as many as possible is good as it increases your chances of attracting the attention of more people towards. Begin with having a presence on one or two social networks and gradually build your way up.

3: Enroll For A Marketing Course e.g. A Degree On Online Marketing

If you have the budget and time, I'd recommend that you pursue a course in online marketing such as a diploma or a degree to help you build a strong foundation that sets you up for massive success.

If you cannot enroll for formal training, you could enroll for specific internet marketing courses to help you get your footing. You can check out some of the courses on HubSpot or Google.

4: Familiarize Yourself with Internet Analysis

Being able to carry out analysis is essential if you want to become a pro at online marketing. You need to know how to analyze the market and its response towards different strategies to become more aware of its needs so you can incorporate the right strategies in your online marketing plan.

For that, you need to first determine who your target market is. First, be clear on what good or service you will be selling or marketing if you just plan to be a marketer and not the business owner yourself. Once you are clear on who your target market is, find out what percentage of them buys stuff online. Also, find out the platform they use most to find the product. This knowledge will help you to understand where you will sell the product in order to create more awareness about the product you are marketing. For instance, if you are targeting teenage girls who use Facebook and Instagram mostly, you need to have an active presence on these platforms if you really want to generate leads and perhaps make some sales.

Also, determine your major online competitors so you know how they work and market their goods/ services and the size of their online market share. You can do that by signing up for their newsletters, researching their press releases and determining their weaknesses and strengths through their social media accounts, website and blog. You can even purchase an item or two from them to better understand their sales process.

5: Interpret the Gathered Data and Create a Strategy

Next, create reports with the help of Google Analytics, spreadsheets or any other good software using the data you have gathered. Use your reports and the results to create a successful marketing strategy that helps you to better reach your target market. Whatever your strategy is, you will need to create some content for it. If you have developed the copywriting skill that we discussed earlier, you won't have much trouble in creating written content on your own. However, if you don't have a lot of time to get the work done and want to create other types of content like infographics, you can hire freelancers from the different freelancing sites mentioned above such as Upwork.com, Freelancer.com, Fiverr.com etc.

Once you have a strategy, implement it and use Google Analytics to determine its effectiveness since this is the only way to figure out your ROI (return on investment). Analyze your strengths and weaknesses and then bring changes to your strategy accordingly to enhance its effectiveness.

As you work on these strategies to become better at online marketing, do build the habit of interacting with people and making more and better social networks.

Next, we will discuss why this is important:

Why you Need to Build the Habit of Having Lots of Social Networks

Networking is an essential skill if you want to succeed in any profession. However, its importance increases if you are trying to increase sales through online marketing. Naturally, the more people you know, the better will be the chances of more people getting connected with your business and skyrocketing its sales.

Also, having more people in your social network helps you to build strong valuable contacts that can help you to attain different goals, which you wouldn't attain if you didn't have a large social network. For instance, if you know someone who is good at creating websites or knows coding, you can learn the skill from him/ her for free or at a discount, or ask them to create your business website for free or at a special price. Not only that, but by knowing more people, you get a chance to know their social networks better too and leverage them in the hour of need.

To build this good habit, you have to start reaching out to all the people you know on different social media sites and even otherwise. Have some quick chitchat if you can so you understand what it is they could be expecting from your brand or you as a person. Just sharing what you do to everyone who cares to listen or pay attention is a good first step, as it will undoubtedly open opportunities referrals. For instance, if you reach out to your friends on various networks and tell them that you are an online marketing expert, some may want to give you jobs to help them get their businesses off the ground, some may want you to train them for a fee, some may want to refer you to their friends etc. This ultimately benefits you more than you could have imagined.

The fourth skill that can help you earn in six figures is being great at closing sales. The next chapter talks about it.

DOWNLOAD YOUR FREE BONUS:

Pursue Your Passion E-book

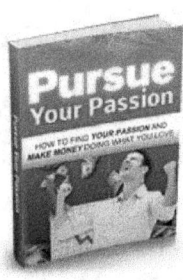

http://bit.ly/PursueYourPassionNow

Chapter 5: Skill #4- Build Great Selling Skills

Life is about selling; we are always selling ourselves in one way or the other. Whether you are selling yourself to prospective spouses, employers, clients or customers, you are always selling yourself- it doesn't matter whether there is monetary consideration to the process. If you sell yourself short, you can be sure that you will definitely not get as many benefits as you would if you were good at it. That's why it is important to be purposeful about building the selling skill if you want to convert it to a moneymaking skill.

To earn 6 figures, you need to take your work to the next level. Whether you are running your own business or working for someone else, if you are good at selling, you can easily use this skill to earn big bucks fast. Before discussing this skill, let us quickly establish the difference between sales and marketing so you don't confuse the two as often, both the terms are used interchangeably which makes them difficult to understand.

Difference between Sales And Marketing

Marketing refers to promoting goods and services and bringing them closer to the target market. Selling, on the other hand refers to actually selling those goods and services i.e. closing deals to move the customer from a prospective customer to a real customer. The job of a marketer is to carry out research on a certain service or product, explore its target markets, map out the price points based on different business factors, brand the services and goods, develop as well as analyze campaigns and then help the salespeople comprehend the unique selling proposition for every product. Salespeople take it up from there. A salesperson serves as the connection between a marketer and the potential customers. A salesperson actually sells the product to the potential customers and uses his/her knowledge of the product as well as knowledge about the target market's needs and demographics to lure potential customers towards a good or service and then make a sale.

Since you don't need to directly speak to the customer in online marketing, you work as both a salesperson and marketer when carrying it out. However, if you are physically selling a product or have a physical presence of your business, you need to build good selling skills.

Why is this skill important? Let's discuss that:

Importance of Building Good Selling Skills

Good salesman ship is important for a number of reasons.

Firstly, it helps you get directly in touch with the potential customers and draw their attention towards the product. If you are good at selling stuff, you will easily grasp the attention of potential customers and turn them into actual customers.

If you are running your own business, building this skill is important so you can then hire and train others to effectively sell your products/services as your business expands. Even if you are not running your own business, but are working in the sales department or any other department of a company, you need to know how to sell things. If you are in the sales department, selling is your job and being good at it will naturally increase chances of your promotion and success. However, if you are in some other department, having good selling skills will help you increase your popularity in the firm and come in the limelight. When people spread the word that they purchased a product or got to know of a business because of you, you will earn more recognition in the company and this will undoubtedly put you perfectly on the path to six figure income.

Not only that, but good sales skills help you sell your talents and skills better too. If you know the art of selling, you can easily promote your skills and talents in a gathering and draw the attention of relevant people towards your work. For instance, if you are engaging with people who work at a big company and want to work as a copywriter for them, you need to convince them of your excellent capabilities. If you are a good salesperson, you will do this job successfully and bag good clients.

To cap it all, selling things effectively helps you progress better in different areas of your business. Let us find out how you can build and improve this skill.

How to Become a Good Salesperson

Here are some effective ways to build good selling skills.

1: Be Clear on Your Mission

Start off by clarifying your mission. What niche do you want to venture in? What will you sell? Who is your target market and what are their needs? How can your product/service satisfy their needs? How much does your target market earn? What is your professional goal?

Answer these questions to better understand your goal and mission in life. This shouldn't just be when identifying your sales mission, but also your goals in different aspects of your life. Successful people across the world have the habit of setting clear and meaningful goals for themselves. This is precisely what helps them understand their goals, become passionate about them and then actively pursue such goals. Therefore, you need to figure out exactly what you want in different areas of your life such as health, wealth, abundance, fitness, spirituality, love etc. and then set meaningful goals based on those findings. This will help you to clearly understand your wants and needs, and then pursue them.

Therefore, spend quality time with yourself every day and analyze your deepest and genuine desires, interests, likes, passions and strengths to better understand what you want and then pursue it.

2: Set Specific Sales Goals

Once you are clear on your sales related mission, break it down into yearly, monthly, weekly and daily goals so you know exactly what you should sell every day to fulfill your mission. Your goals should be results based such as sales per month, profit per sale, amount per sale etc. so they can help you measure your progress easily.

3: Understand Your Customers' Needs

Find out what your target market wants from your product/service to better understand its need. Engage with your potential customers on a regular basis through social media, through email or by calling them if you can. Also, conduct surveys to find out what your target market expects from your business or why they prefer your competitor's product/ service over yours.

4: Have a Compelling Sales Pitch

Create a striking sales pitch that focuses on the importance and benefits of your product/service and how it can solve a particular problem or fulfill the need of your target market. Practice that pitch as much as you can and make sure it is concise and to-the-point. Next, start delivering it whenever you feel you are around someone who may be interested in your product/service.

Also, increase your social networks because the more people you know, the better will be your chances of making more sales.

Another skill that is worth building is being good at managing teams. The next chapter throws light on it.

DOWNLOAD YOUR FREE BONUS:

Pursue Your Passion E-book

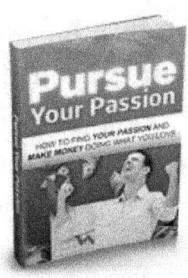

http://bit.ly/PursueYourPassionNow

Chapter 6: Skill #5- Having Good Management Skills

Let's be honest, pulling six figures a month without needing any help from anybody is not going to be easy. In fact, it is bad practice if you shoulder all the burden. What if you get sick or are just not able to get the work done for one reason or another; does that mean you will make zero income? That's where teams come in.

Whether you are running your own business or working for someone, if you have good team management skills, you can easily take your business to the next level, improve its overall performance and sales, and start earning 6 figures.

Let's find out right here why you need to build good team management skills and how you can achieve this goal.

The Need to Build Good Management Skills

Management skills are all the skills that help you manage your team members and those working under or around you effectively. If you are a good manager, you understand your team better and can work as a good liaison between them and your superiors.

When you effectively communicate what clients, bosses and other stakeholders want, this makes it easy for those working under you to take appropriate action to do what needs to be done in the manner in which it should be done. The fact that there is clear communication eliminates ambiguity and confusion, which ultimately keeps everyone happy. The same applies if you are running your own business. Being able to understand your team helps you exploit their strengths better and keep them more engaged in their work.

Moreover, good management skills help you resolve problems easily and guide your team in an effective manner. You ensure everyone is on the same page with you and take each member together as a team to make them work zealously for you or your company. This improves the overall performance of the organization.

If you too want your business or the company you are working for to become better than ever, you must purpose to build/improve your management skills. How do you do that? Here is how:

How to Improve Your Management Skills

To become better at managing teams, you first need to know the members in your team. Only when you know your team, can you understand the needs, potentials and qualities of different members. Finding out their needs helps you know what they are seeking from your company so you can help them reach their goals, which ultimately helps them to feel more motivated to give their best to the organization. Becoming aware of their talents, skills and potentials helps you know of their personal assets that you can exploit successfully and make your team members more involved in your work.

Secondly, you need to start engaging with your team members as much as you can. Talk to them in the workplace and even outside of it to build a good rapport with them. The more comfortable they are talking to you, the easier it will be for you to influence them and make them work effectively for you.

Thirdly, you need to communicate your concerns and message to them effectively. The key to doing that is to inform them of their responsibilities so they know what is expected of them and how a certain project is expected to grow.

Fourthly, you need to lead by example by practicing what you preach. If you ask your team members to do a certain thing or behave a certain way, you must do that yourself. When your team sees you practicing what you preach, they are likely to follow your example.

As you become a better manager and build good management skills, you could create courses on team management or give lectures to prospective and budding managers to improve their management skills. This will help you use your management skills to earn some good side income and improve your chances of earning six figures. If you do venture into this, building good public skills will definitely help you out. The next chapter elaborates on that.

Chapter 7: Skill #6- Build Effective Public Speaking Skills

Renowned public speakers like Tony Robbins, Jack Canfield and Brian Tracy earn millions of dollars each year with the help of their public speaking skills. Besides these brilliant speakers, there are many people who make hundreds of thousands of dollars through public speaking.

What does it entail? And why is it important to build the skill anyway? Let's discuss that:

Public Speaking and its Importance

Public speaking is simply that; speaking in public/before an audience regarding a certain topic of interest to the audience. While you may not perceive it to be a million dollar making skill, this skill can most certainly help you reach your goal of financial abundance and prosperity. If you are good at public speaking, you can become a keynote speaker and speak at different institutes. Keynote speakers usually earn anywhere between $10,000 and $100,000 for just a one hour lecture. Even if you are earning around $5,000 per every keynote, you only need about 20 bookings to earn 6 figures annually.

However, to reach this point, you will first need to take public speaking seriously and build good speaking skills.

Moreover, you can speak in seminars and workshops, and even give public speaking training sessions to increase your income. You can also create your own products and sell them to further boost up your income. For instance, Brain Tracy has created many public speaking programs and makes thousands of dollars each year by selling them. Tony Robbins is known to organize 'A Date With Destiny', which he charges over $5000 per person for attendance.

In addition, you can also give coaching lessons to other speakers especially the budding speakers to help them improve their skill and make some more money through this venture. However, this will only be possible when you have earned enough recognition and popularity through public speaking.

Here is how you can build this skill.

How to Become a Good Public Speaker

To become an excellent public speaker, first narrow down on a topic you would like to speak about. You need to have a certain area of expertise that you can speak effectively on. Unless you figure that out, it is likely you won't have a clear public speaking goal and strategy and won't be able to find your true voice. For instance, Tony Robbins is a motivational speaker and his job is to motivate people to be better. Similarly, Grand Cardone is a huge sales giant who ventured into public speaking some time back. He talks mainly about how to become a good salesman and that's his area of expertise.

Similarly, you have to find out what you are passionate about because if you are truly passionate about something, you will find it effortless to speak on it and improve your knowledge about that area.

Secondly, find your target market so you can research better on its needs and requirements. Next, you need to set your fee. Find out what your competitors are charging for an hour long talk to set a suitable price for your speaking engagements.

Next, you need to look for good speaking venues or engagements where you can meet people and speak to them. This helps you make more contacts and use them to sell your service better or to convince them of what you talk about. As you have more funds to rent halls and other venues to hold seminars, speaking events and workshops, start creating your events so you can sell your knowledge to people. Also, work on building your online presence so you can reach out to more people (you could for instance create a YouTube channel to help you to generate leads for you speaking engagements).

The seventh skill you should consider building is graphic designing. The last chapter of the book talks about it.

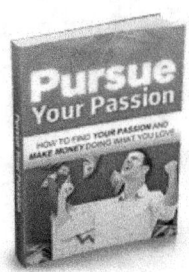

Chapter 8: Skill #7- Learn Graphic Designing

Graphic design is the science and art of creating and arranging different text and images to communicate a certain message. It can be applied in different media such as digital, print, motion picture, product decoration, animation, signs and packaging. It is one of the most trending skills nowadays and is definitely one that can help you earn six figures.

I know you might be wondering; why is this skill so important anyway? Let's discuss that:

Importance of Graphic Designing

It is quite common for graphic designers these days to make anywhere between $35,000 and $65,000 annually. This amount increases as your experience and expertise improves. In fact, there are many successful graphic designers who are earning 6 figures per year, as employees in various companies and as freelancers.

Moreover, you can also teach graphic designing when you become good at it and hold seminars to earn extra income. If you are running your own business, graphic designing can help you create a good layout and design of your business website as well as more creative designs for your products and services.

Here is how you can become a skilled graphic designer.

How to Build the Graphic Designing Skill

Here are a few ways to build and improve your design skills.

- You could take different online tutorials and courses to learn the art of graphic designing and improve this skill. Here are some great tutorials that you can follow to learn graphics designing.

- Read lots of design books and follow different graphics design blogs to become up-to-date with the latest trends and to improve your knowledge of this skill. Designrfix, Gainbuzz, DesignTaxi and Artwork Abode are some good design blogs that can teach you how to build and improve this skill. A few good design books to begin with are: The Elements of Typographic Style by Robert Bringhurst, Graphic Design Theory: Readings from the Field by Helen Armstrong and 100 Ideas that Changed Graphic Design by Steven

Heller. In addition, work on building the habit of reading good informational and how-to books regularly. Reading is one good habit all accomplished people possess that has helped them earn millions of dollars.

- As you learn the basics of graphic design, create some designs and create your portfolio or a few samples to show potential clients. And as you do that, make sure to practice as much as possible to enhance your skill.

- To take it a notch higher, create your profile on different online platforms like Upwork.com, Fiverr.com, Freelancer.com, 99designs.com etc. (these have been mentioned earlier on in the book) then apply for different graphics design jobs.

Work on these tips, stay consistent in your work and interact more with people to increase your chances of finding better, bigger clients.

DOWNLOAD YOUR FREE BONUS:

Pursue Your Passion E-book

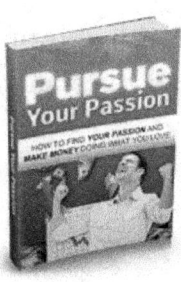

http://bit.ly/PursueYourPassionNow

Conclusion

We have come to the end of the book. Thank you for reading and congratulations for reading until the end.

I hope this book provided you with the value you were looking for and helps you achieve your goal of earning a 6 figure income.

If you found the book valuable, can you recommend it to others? One way to do that is to post a review on Amazon.

Click here to leave a review for this book on Amazon!

Thank you and good luck!

Passive Income

7 Predictable Ways to Generate a Passive Income Stream when you are over 40 and While Working a Full Time Job

Introduction

I want to thank you and congratulate you for downloading the book, *"Passive Income: 7 Predictable Ways to Generate a Passive Income Stream While Working a Full Time Job"*.

This book has actionable information on 7 predictable ways through which you can generate passive income while retaining your full-time job.

A passive income is any income earned from income streams that do not need consistent every day input. Traditionally, many used the term"passive income" in reference to income earned from investment vehicles such as stocks, dividends, rent, interest on monies, royalties, capital gains, etc. Thanks to technology, this definition has morphed.

Today, while the definition of a passive income still remains the same, income generated from sources that do not require consistent output, in light of a society entrenched in working a day job for 8 or more hours 5 days a week, any income generated from working 2-3 hours a day can fit into the passive income description.

Because of this and other reasons such as financial and time freedom, supplementation of income, unlimited income potential, and most importantly, being the 'boss,' creating a passive income stream to supplement, or even replace an active income has become the "it-thing" and thousands of people are now looking for ways to earn a passive income while working a day job.

Since you are reading this, undoubtedly, you would like to learn how to earn a passive income as a way to supplement your active income, or earn enough to leave the confines of your day job.

If this is what you desire, you're in luck because the internet has made the prospect easier and unlike days gone, to get started, you don't need thousands of dollars. All you need is a computer (or even a smartphone), and active internet connection, and 2-3 hours of your day for no less than 3 months. After this time (which is often how long it takes to setup an online-based, passive income-generating stream), you can work for as little as 4 hours a week and still earn well enough to quit your day job if you so wish.

In this book, we are going to discuss 7 highly potent, yet relatively easy to implement, online-based passive income streams you can implement while working a day job since they require minimal hours to setup (2-3 consistent hours per day).

The good thing about these passive income streams is that when you successfully implement one, you can move on to the others, and by so doing, create multiple passive income streams that take less than 4 hours per week to manage.

Thanks again for downloading this book. I hope you enjoy it!

Table of Contents

I won't go round in circles trying to justify why you should venture into passive income because given that you are reading this book, you perhaps have heard great things about passive income e.g. ease of scalability, the passive nature of the income, tax benefits etc., which has informed your decision to look out for ways to make passive income. Instead, we will immediately start by discussing the different strategies you can follow to make passive income in a step by step format.

1st Strategy: Blogging

Blogging is the most common and predictable way to earn a passive income. In fact, many of the other sources of online passive income anchor on blogs. In other words, if you have a blog that has a good enough readership, you can start and support almost all the other online passive income strategies that we will be discussing in this book.

Since you're not new to the internet, you have read success stories of bloggers such as Brett McKay of artofmanliness.com, John Chow of Johnchow.com, Mario Lavandeira of PerezHilton.com, and Pat Flynn of Smartpassiveincome.com, and other bloggers who earn thousands of dollars per month from blogging about topics and things they love. This goes to show you just how powerful blogging is as an income stream.

The good thing about blogging is that to get started, you need nothing but a passion, dedication (the willingness to dedicate 2-3 hours of your day to blogging), and a bit of easy to learn technical knowledge (which is where this book comes in). Here is how to go about it:

How to Start a Revenue-Generating Blog

In this guide, we are going to reveal how to use your free time (in the morning before heading to your day job or in the evening—morning works best because as Pat Flynn says, "always start your day by dedicating 2 hours to working for yourself) to create a blog that generates no less than $1,000 per month. Let's get to it:

Step 1: Choose a Topic/Niche

To set up a successful blog that earns you a passive income going into hundreds of thousands of dollars as you work your other job, sleep, or even travel, the first thing you need to do is choose a topic. Here, go with a topic that impassions you because at the end of the day, blogging should be fun and because it takes time to bear fruit—do not expect to make tons of money a month after starting—passion is a key ingredient because it ensures you stick to blogging when quitting seems like the best option.

With that said however, research from Wpromote shows that the top 5 most popular blog categories are music, fashion, travel, food, and beauty. While this also means these are the most competitive, you are free to go with what you feel most passionate about. At the end of the day, even if you chose a less competitive topic that does not impassion you, your chances of creating an income generating blog are very minimal since the prospect calls for patience and a lot of dedication. Once you have your topic of interest at hand...

Step 2: Choose a Domain and Hosting Option for Your Site

As indicated earlier, the greatest thing about blogging is that you do not need to invest anything other than your time; this is because if you choose to, you can use hosted blog option such as blogger.com, wordpress.com, or even squarespace.com. The downside to using these options is that while the hosting is free, the domain name is not brandable.

For instance, if you decide to create a blog about a specific genre of music such as reggae, and you choose to name your blog "one love reggae," if you go with the WordPress option, your domain name shall be "onelovereggae.wordpress.com. This, as you can see, is a mouthful. On the other hand, a self-hosted blog allows you to choose a brandable domain. Using the reggae example, the domain name would be onelovereggae.com. You can learn how to choose a domain name here.

A domain will cost you anywhere from $1-$15 per year while hosting will vary depending on the provider and the option you choose (BlueHost, iPage and HostGator have options starting from as little as $3 per month). This article has some great insight on how to settle on a hosting provider.

You shall also need to setup your blog and customize it as you see fit. Google these things—you will find tons of related information related to your chosen blogging platform. For instance, if you opt to use WordPress, the world's most popular blogging platform, you can get ideas on how to set up your WordPress blog from Siteground.com or WPbeginner.com.

Step 3: Start Writing and Driving Traffic to Your Blog

With your blog all set up, the next step is to start writing content. In the online space, content reigns supreme. This is because how unique, informational, and helpful to readers it is, and how well optimized it is for search bots will determine how popular your blog becomes and how much traffic it generates. More traffic equals more money potential.

When it comes to deciding what to blog about, your passion should come in handy and help you brainstorm topics. In terms of driving traffic to your blog, concentrate on being super helpful to readers by writing amazing content, and then optimize this content for search engines. This therefore means you have to conduct keyword research and use this to write for people and optimize your content for search. This is not as difficult as it sounds and with CMS (content management systems) such as WordPress, you will find tons of plugins (such as SEO Yoast) that shall help you with search engine optimization.

Another thing you should do here is create an editorial calendar so you avoid the mistake of blogging when you feel like it. Creating a revenue generating blog require consistency.

Brainstorm 50-100 blog ideas and spread them out on calendar (aim for a blog a day since research has shown that frequently updated blogs attract more traffic).

Step 4: Monetize

When your blog starts attracting visitors, you are free to monetize it by creating products related to your blog. For instance, if your blog is on reggae, you can create a reggae guitar guide for beginners eBook), affiliate marketing, or make money with advertisements from ad networks like Chitika, Media.net, , Ad Maven, Vibrant Media, Clicksor, Advertising.com, Google Adsense, , Revenue Hits, Revcontent, AdBlade, Undertone, , PropellerAds, WWW Promoter, Infolinks, Adbuff etc. or targeted ads from companies fit your audience. As I already mentioned, many of the other blog monetization options like selling software, mobile apps, selling physical products, independent publishing, membership sites, information courses etc. can be anchored on a blog so make sure to take blogging seriously if you really want to end up making real money from blogging. The opportunities for making passive income when you have a blog are endless! Monetization options for a traffic generating blog are endless and once you get consistent traffic, you will have your fair share of picks.

More important than monetizing is making sure the blog is helpful to readers and friendly to search engines.

As you shall note, the other strategies we shall discuss here shall depend on how well you can implement this one strategy because without a blog/website, the other strategies shall be less effective.

To help you out further, here are various resources related to creating an income-generating blog:

How to choose a niche for your blog

http://www.bloggingwizard.com

http://www.wpsuperstars.net

How to set up a WordPress blog (WordPress is the easiest to use CMS)

http://www.wpbeginner.com

How to drive traffic to a blog

http://neilpatel.com

https://www.iwillteachyoutoberich.com

DOWNLOAD YOUR FREE BONUS:

<u>5 PASSIVE INCOME BUSINESS MODELS VIDEO COURSE</u>

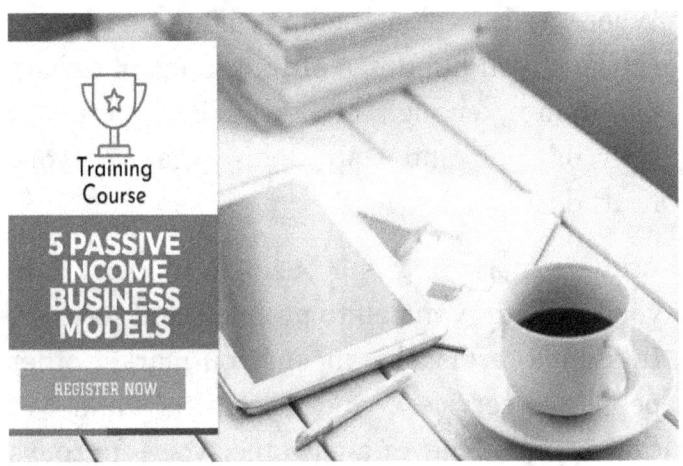

https://quintons-school.teachable.com/

2nd Strategy: Affiliate Marketing

Affiliate marketing is an amazing way to generate a gushing stream of passive income. When well implemented, affiliate marketing can earn you hundreds of thousands of dollars per month, enough money to have you quit your day job and start doing whatever your heart desires.

Affiliate marketing is a business model where you "affiliate" yourself to products and services. In simple terms, this means you market other peoples' services and products and in exchange, whenever a customer you refer buys a product or service, you earn a percentage of the buying price. For instance, if you refer someone to a piece of software retailing for $500 and you have an affiliate relationship with the software company stipulating that for every referral, you will earn 20%, you will earn $100.

In the online space, the affiliate marketing business model uses special links called "affiliate links."Affiliate links are unique web links provided to affiliate marketers for marketing purposes. The link has a special cookie unique to you; the purpose of this cookie is to capture where the lead/referral is coming from so that when someone clicks on the link and buys something, the purchase reflects on your referral account and you can receive a commission for it.

Affiliate marketing offers exponential potential. For instance, if you have a popular reggae blog, you can affiliate yourself to reggae concerts sellers, guitar sellers, and other such companies that match your audience needs. You can do all this from the same website because to affiliate yourself, all you have to do is insert a link into a page or a post.

For instance, if you are writing a post title "10 amazing-sounding guitars ideal for reggae music," for each guitar on the list, you can drop an affiliate link to a retailer (make sure you have an affiliate relationship with the retailer), and when someone clicks on your affiliate link and makes a purchase, you shall earn a commission.

To get started on affiliate marketing, create a website or blog using the steps outlined in the previous strategy. Once the blog starts generating traffic on a consistent basis, decide which affiliate offers are a fit for your audience and affiliate yourself to these offers by inserting the affiliate links into your posts and pages. You don't have to have a personal relationship with the companies that are recruiting affiliates. You can register in affiliate marketplaces i.e. websites that help publishers find advertisers. Some of the popular places you can register as an affiliate include the following:

ClickBank

CJ Affiliate by Conversant (Formerly known as Commission Junction)

ShareASale

Amazon Associates

EBay Partner Network

Rakuten Affiliate Network

Avangate

Revenue Wire

TradeDoubler

And many others

In accordance with the law, every time you insert an affiliate link into your content or page, insert a disclaimer letting readers know that by using the affiliate link to make a purchase, you will earn a commission.

Another way to go about affiliate marketing is using paid advertising. For instance, let us assume you would like to affiliate yourself to a "custom guitar" service. You can use paid advertising on platforms such as Google AdWords and social media platforms such as Instagram, Facebook, Twitter, and other paid advertising options to promote the service to the masses.

To be successful at affiliate marketing, and therefore, earn a passive income even as you sleep, you are better off operating from a blog or website because this allows for centralization and diversification. For instance, even when you want to use paid advertising to promote a custom guitar service, you are likely to be more successful if you create a post reviewing the service (from a personal perspective), and then promoting this post on social media. This will ensure that when the service becomes popular, that one post can earn you thousands of dollars year after year without needing any maintenance.

As a rule of thumb, do not affiliate yourself to product or services you do not use because when you do and the service and products you promote fail to work as implied, your reputation will suffer because the internet hates fraudsters. To achieve massive success with affiliate marketing, place your offers at strategic areas of your website and pages.

Let us look at an example:

Assume you have a website that has 50 posts generating 1,000 views per month (total traffic=50,000). Out of this, assume that each page has affiliate offers from different companies offering a $100 product. If your conversation rate is 1% per month (a 1% conversion rate is very easy to achieve), it means out of your 50,000 visitors, 500 will be clicking on your affiliate links and purchasing. If your affiliate relationship with these providers stipulates that you earn 10% of the purchase price, each conversion shall earn you $10 and therefore, you shall earn more than $5, 000 each month.

The affiliate marketing process is as follows:

1. Drive massive amounts of traffic to your website.

2. Find affiliate programs and offers that fit your audience.

3. Insert your affiliate links into your wildly popular posts and pages while making sure that this insertion adds value to readers' lives.

4. Be open about your affiliate relationship by adding an affiliate disclaimer to each affiliate offer.

5. Optimize your conversion rate so you can convert as many of your web visitors as possible.

If you can do the above and find well-paying offers, you will be well on your way to earning money as you commute, travel, work at your day job, or even sleep. What a life!

Further reading

https://www.locationrebel.com

http://nichehacks.com

MonetizePros.com.

http://www.affiliatebible.com

http://www.wpeagle.com

Myworkfromhomemoney.com

NeilPatel.com

3rd Strategy: Membership Sites

A membership site is a blog-like website where members pay a monthly fee to access premium content not freely available on the blog section of the website.

Contrary to popular belief, creating a membership site does not require tons of technical knowledge such as web design or coding because with WordPress, you can use plugins to bar some information and make it available to paying members. One of the greatest things about a membership site is the recurrent nature of the business.

As an example, if the barred content you create for membership site is eBooks, podcasts, video and audio webinars, or virtual conferences, if you keep the information fresh and updated (for example, you offer webinars and conferences on a daily, weekly, or even monthly basis), if you keep the information valuable, paid members will keep paying the membership fee.

To get started, create a website/blog as indicated earlier. For this purpose, you can create WordPress based website (it's easier to manage thanks to plugins and an easy to use interface) and install a membership plugin such as MemberPress or S2member (simply search the plugin on the plugins search bar). The plugin shall guide you through the process of adding the product and payment options. Make sure this information is very relevant your web visitors and compels them to want to pay to join your membership site. Make sure that creating a username and password is easy and seamless too because if the process is not easy, users will be at odds and your conversion rate may suffer. You can also create various levels of membership options.

Creating a successful membership site depends on the following.

The first thing you have to do is build trust: no one wants to buy something from someone he or she does not know or trust. The best way to do this is to offer freebies such as trial or free content. For instance, assuming your website is on self-development, you can create free self-development content for your site as a way to build trust and show readers that if you have such valuable information on your free blog, the information restricted to members is infinitely better. This will make it easier for web visitors to subscribe to your membership and pay the monthly fee.

As obvious as it sounds, the key to success in this venture is to drive traffic to your site (traffic is central to all online-based, passive income strategies discussed here). To ensure you convert these visitors into paid members, create an effective lead magnet. A lead magnetis a bribe in the form of upgrades, freebies, and signup incentives that gets people to give you their contact information such as email and name. For instance, besides the free content, you can offer a free consultation.

Let us look at an example:

Assume you have a members only self-improvement blog where you have three levels: the free level, level one that offers premium content every month, level 2 that offers free content and 2 coaching sessions per month, and level 3 that offers weekly coaching sessions.

Assume that your site attracts 200,000 visitors per month. Out of these, 100,000 go for the free content. Out of the remaining 100,000, you convert 1% (1,000 people) as follows: 950 choose level 1 priced at $49 per month (total=$46,550), 30 choose level 2 priced at $99 per month (total=$2,970), and 20 choose level 3 priced at $299 per month (total=5,980), your total earning shall be $55, 500, which is not bad at all. Since the bulk of this revenue shall be from level 1 that does not require one on one consulting, you can use your weekend to create content for them.

As for the rest, you can schedule them into your calendar accordingly. If you give each of person a 30-minute consulting session and work for 2 hours every day (serving 4 people per day except on weekend), a month shall be enough time to offer premium one-on-one services that leave your client happy.

Once you reach such a point, you can take off the pressure by delegating tasks. For instance, you can outsource the creation of the premium content (after drafting it of course), uploading it to the site, customer service for member response, social media marketing and management, and simply concentrate on offering one on one coaching. This shall help you grow your business to a point where if you so want, you can quit your day job and concentrate on the membership site full time (thereby increasing your earning potential).

The beauty of membership sites is that they work across all niches and as long as people are interested in a specific topic and you can create highly valuable content on the same, you can earn money from it. For instance, you can create a membership site offering premium freelance writing jobs.

Further reading

http://theworldismyoffice.com

http://www.wpbeginner.com

https://www.inc.com

https://ontraport.com

4th Strategy: Kindle Publishing

Of the passive income strategies we shall discuss here, this is the only one that does not necessarily demand a website. And the good news about it is that you can make your first sale as a complete beginner within less than 24 hours!

Publishing books has always been profitable; so profitable in fact, that traditional publishers are constantly giving new writers book advances running into seven figures. The good news is that to create a publishing empire, you do not necessarily need to go the traditional publishing way especially considering that getting a publisher is not a stroll in the park. You can self-publish on Kindle.

Kindle publishing (Kindle Direct Publishing) is the publishing arm of technology giant Amazon. Launched in 2007, KDP as its abbreviated helps authors independently publish their book to Amazon's 193 million monthly visitors.

Kindle publishing, like affiliate marketing, offers unlimited potential especially if you are looking to publish more than one book (which you should if you want to earn thousands of dollars from the prospect). Here is everything you need to know about creating a passive income-generating kindle publishing empire:

Step 1: Choose a Niche

Your success as a Kindle publisher shall depend on your ability to find profitable niches topics on which to write books. The great thing here is that to do so, you need not look further than Amazon. No matter how great a writer you are, if you write a book on a topic that lacks readership, topic readers' want solutions to, you will be shooting yourself in the foot.

Here, the easiest thing you can do is think of a problem you would like to solve. Here is a secret no other passive income book shall tell you: ***if you are truly committed to creating lasting streams of passive income, you have to solve a problem people are willing to pay to solve***.

Once you have a problem in mind, visit the Kindle Best seller site. On the left hand side, you are going to see categories. Choose a category you think you can write a book on (or one that matches the problem you want to solve). If you are yet to decide which problem to tackle, simply choose a category you consider appealing.

When you navigate to a specific category, you will head deeper into that category and you may find other sub-categories. For instance, if you decide to go with self-help, under it, you will see other sub-categories such as creativity, eating disorders, happiness, etc. Choose one you want to scrutinize further and keep digging until you get to the sub niches.

As an example, below are the top 100 books in the niche self-help and sub-niche eating disorder and body image. Once you're in the bestseller niche and sub-niche, look for patterns. Can you notice 2 or more books on related topics? If you notice 2 or more books on a related topic, this is an indicator that this topic is popular and doing well.

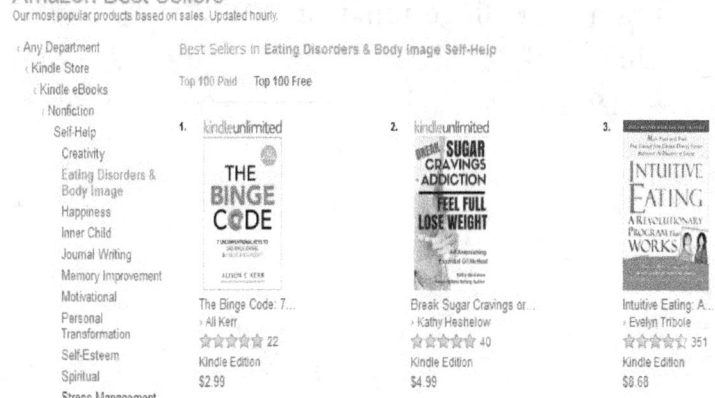

The next step is to dig further. Amazon Kindle ranks books according to their download and reviews. A popular and often downloaded book will have a higher rank with 1 being the most downloaded book.

When you notice related books, click on each book (you can open different tabs on your browser), and then scroll down; you will see the book rank. For instance, from the above, we see that binge eating is a popular topic because at the time of writing this, the 1st book (Binge eating code), the 4th book (brain over binge), and several other books (3rd, 9th, 13th, 14th, and several others) are on the list of 100.

The next step is to open some of these books to see their rank. At the time of writing this, Binge eating code ranks at 14, 477 in the entire Kindle store. Intuitive eating ranks at 17, 374, and Brain over Binge ranks at 18,168 respectively. This rank changes every minute (Amazon updates it every 6 hours).

Product details

File Size: 3740 KB
Print Length: 188 pages
Page Numbers Source ISBN: 1999786408
Simultaneous Device Usage: Unlimited
Publisher: MindFree; 1 edition (July 6, 2017)
Publication Date: July 6, 2017
Sold by: Amazon Digital Services LLC
Language: English
ASIN: B073HDB6ZN
Text-to-Speech: Enabled ⌄
X-Ray: Not Enabled ⌄
Word Wise: Enabled
Lending: Not Enabled
Enhanced Typesetting: Not Enabled ⌄
Amazon Best Sellers Rank: #14,477 Paid in Kindle Store (See Top 100 Paid in Kindle Store)

    #1 in Kindle Store > Kindle eBooks > Nonfiction > Self-Help > **Eating Disorders & Body Image**
    #9 in Books > Health, Fitness & Dieting > Mental Health > **Eating Disorders**
    #36 in Kindle Store > Kindle eBooks > Health, Fitness & Dieting > Diets & Weight Loss > Diets > **Weight Maintenance**

Product details

File Size: 3297 KB
Print Length: 369 pages
Page Numbers Source ISBN: 1250004047
Publisher: St. Martin's Griffin; 3 edition (August 7, 2012)
Publication Date: August 7, 2012
Sold by: Amazon Digital Services LLC
Language: English
ASIN: B006ZL3P4G
Text-to-Speech: Enabled ⌄
X-Ray: Enabled ⌄
Word Wise: Enabled
Lending: Not Enabled
Screen Reader: Supported ⌄
Enhanced Typesetting: Enabled ⌄
Amazon Best Sellers Rank: #17,374 Paid in Kindle Store (See Top 100 Paid in Kindle Store)

    #3 in Kindle Store > Kindle eBooks > Nonfiction > Self-Help > **Eating Disorders & Body Image**
    #5 in Kindle Store > Kindle eBooks > Medical eBooks > Special Topics > **Nutrition**
    #13 in Books > Health, Fitness & Dieting > Mental Health > **Eating Disorders**

Product details

File Size: 1215 KB
Print Length: 328 pages
Publisher: Camellia Publishing (January 1, 2011)
Publication Date: January 1, 2011
Sold by: Amazon Digital Services LLC
Language: English
ASIN: B005F9UZ1U
Text-to-Speech: Enabled
X-Ray: Enabled
Word Wise: Enabled
Lending: Not Enabled
Screen Reader: Supported
Enhanced Typesetting: Enabled
Amazon Best Sellers Rank: #18,168 Paid in Kindle Store (See Top 100 Paid in Kindle Store)
  #4 in Kindle Store > Kindle eBooks > Nonfiction > Self-Help > Eating Disorders & Body Image
  #15 in Books > Health, Fitness & Dieting > Mental Health > Eating Disorders
  #214 in Kindle Store > Kindle eBooks > Biographies & Memoirs > Memoirs

The idea here is to look for related books that are ranking well. If several related books rank at 1>20,000, this is a niche worth pursuing; it means the book ranking at 20,000 is selling a minimum of 3-15 books per day. The screenshot below shows the Kindle rank in relation to book sales and potential incomes.

- ✓ Rank 50,000 to 100,000— selling 0— 1 book a day.

- ✓ Rank 10,000 to 50,000— selling 3 to 15 books a day.

- ✓ **Rank 5,500 to 10,000— selling 15 to 30 books a day.**

- ✓ Rank 3,000 to 5,500— selling 30 to 50 books a day.

- ✓ ***Rank 500 to 3,000— selling 50 to 200 books a day***

- ✓ Rank 350 to 500— selling 200 to 300 books a day.

- ✓ Rank 100 to 350— selling 300 to 500 books a day.

- ✓ Rank 35 to 100— selling 500 to 1,000 books a day.

- ✓ Rank 10 to 35— selling 1,000 to 2,000 books a day.

- ✓ Rank of 5 to 10— selling 2,000 to 4,000 books a day.

- ✓ Rank of 1 to 5— selling 4,000 + books a day.

Once you find a niche, you have to come up with a title and subtitle for your book and then brainstorm and mindmap your ideas for the book. Fully flesh the mind map until you have a table of content like structure for your book.

Step 2: Write the Book, Create Cover, and Publish

With your mind map at hand, you will notice that your book will most likely write itself and from there, you can dedicate yourself to writing 1,000 words of your book per day. In about 10 days, you will have a publish-worthy book. Once done with the first draft, edit the book a first, second, and third time; if possible, hire an editor. Talking about hiring someone to write your book:

The most amazing thing about the Kindle publishing strategy is that even if you are not the creative type, you can hire someone to write the book for you. You will find great freelancers on site such as Upwork.com, Freelancer.com, WriteArticlesForMe.com, EpicWrite.com, TheWritingSummit.com and other platforms.

Once the book is ready, hire someone to create a book cover on Fiverr.com (or do it yourself if you have the expertise), sign up for Kindle Publishing, and follow the prompts to publish your book.

Step 3: Market the Book

Like most passive income businesses, how much you end up earning from Kindle publishing will depend on how much traffic you can drive to your book. The more exposure your book gets, the better it is likely to perform and the more revenue you are bound to generate.

To market your book, you can use options such as social media, free and paid book promos, paid advertising, guest blogging, and other such ideas.

Let us look at an example:

Assume you create 5 great books that rank at 10,000. This means you shall be selling 15 books of each title each day. Depending on your price point (how you price the book—go for nothing below $2.99 so you can take 70% of the revenue share), you shall be earning $156.957 from the five books per day (70/100 X $ 2.99= $2.093 X 15 books sold each day X 5 book titles= $156.957 per day). This therefore means on a good month, you can take home $4000+. This is not bad considering the effort and the fact that after publishing the book, marketing it will require less than 30 minutes per day.

Further reading

https://kindlepreneur.com

http://okdork.com

https://www.tckpublishing.com

https://www.thecreativepenn.com

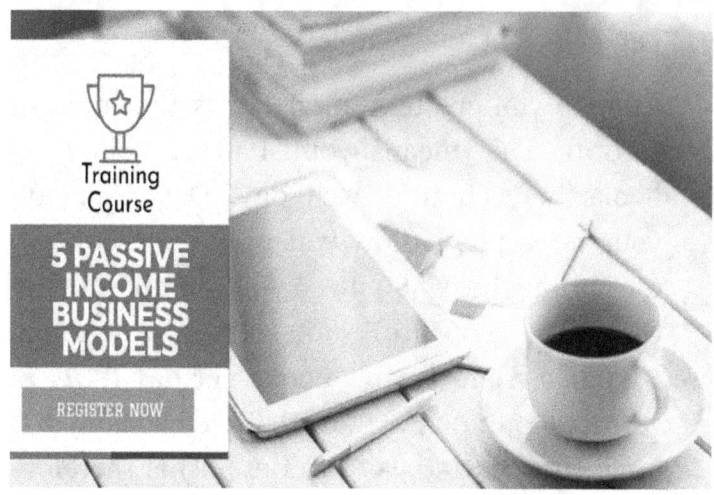

https://quintons-school.teachable.com/

5th Strategy: YouTube Videos

Never before has man loved video than he does now. Today, videos are the most consumed form of online content. From funny cat videos, to game walkthroughs, to makeup videos, video is the "it-thing." And in the world of video, nothing beats YouTube.

Owned by Google, and boasting of over 30 million visitors per day, YouTube is a prime way to generate a passive income. How do you go about this? What do you need to do to become a YouTube millionaire? Let us discuss this:

Step 1: Setup Your Account and Start Creating Content

This one is very straightforward: create an account on YouTube. The process is very straightforward, as all you need is a Google Account. As you do so, however, you may want to pay attention to the nature of your YouTube channel (the topics you shall be covering) and if possible, have the name reflect on the title of your channel. For instance, if you intend to create videos that motivate people, you could name your channel something along the lines of "dailymotivation."

When thinking about which types of videos to create, remember to follow your passion or ask yourself a question such as "what do I know and can teach easily?" This will help you come up with an idea for a channel. The idea here is simple: come up with a channel people will find helpful; this does not necessarily mean that the channel and the videos you create have to be educational. Always remember that if people are actively searching for specific information, you can create video content for it irrespective of whether what they are searching for is funny videos or even weird videos.

When you start creating content, make sure the content is valuable enough to attract views and shares. As an example, the world seems to like videos of "unboxing/reviewing products." If you can buy niche products (products such as vapes), unbox them, and then show people how to use them, you have something on your hands, provided the videos you create are clear and helpful. The good thing about creating YouTube videos is that if you cannot afford expensive shooting cameras, you can get started with the camera on your high-end smartphone.

Step 2: Drive Traffic to the Channel/Video

After creating 10 or 20 videos and uploading them to your channel (do this immediately after creating your channel and before you start promoting it), hit the road and start marketing your channel and the specific videos you have created. The best way to do this is to share the videos on social media (you can even use paid advertising to promote the video to its relevant target audience), or share the video on your blog (see how they two relate?).

The following resources shall teach you optimize your channel for search as well as how to promote your YouTube channel:

https://blog.hootsuite.com

https://www.outbrain.com

Step 3: Monetize

After building your fan and subscriber base and reached 10,000 per video, add monetization to your channel to start making money. Monetizing YouTube is relatively easy because all you have to do is allow Google to serve ads on your channel/videos (the material has to be non-copyrighted).

The monetization option is on your YouTube sidebar on the channel, status, and features option (you have to be logged is as a YouTube publisher). From here, simply enable monetization.

Once you have this setup, you are ready to start earning from YouTube. Let us look at an example:

YouTube pays through Google AdSense through a CPM (cost per Mille or cost per thousand). This means they pay for every 1,000-ad impressions. The CPM for each impression may be $0.1 to $10 depending on the niche you are serving.

Here is how the math would look if we go with a $0.1 CPM:

1,000 views=$0.1

10,000 views=$1

100,000 views=$10

1,000,000 views=$100

10,000,000 views=$1,000

100,000,000 views=$10,000

1,000,000,000 views=$100,000

As you can see, how much you end up earning from YouTube will depend on your ad impression, which shall depend on how many views you can drive to your website; therefore, the more traffic you drive to your channel and videos, the higher the earning potential.

One of the greatest thing about YouTube is that once the video is live and generating views, the multiplication factor is great and in most instances, the video shall market itself (especially if it's good) through person-to-person sharing and social shares:

Further reading

https://www.quora.com

https://www.entrepreneur.com

https://creatoracademy.youtube.com

https://monetizepros.com

https://www.incomediary.com

DOWNLOAD YOUR FREE BONUS:

5 PASSIVE INCOME BUSINESS
MODELS VIDEO COURSE

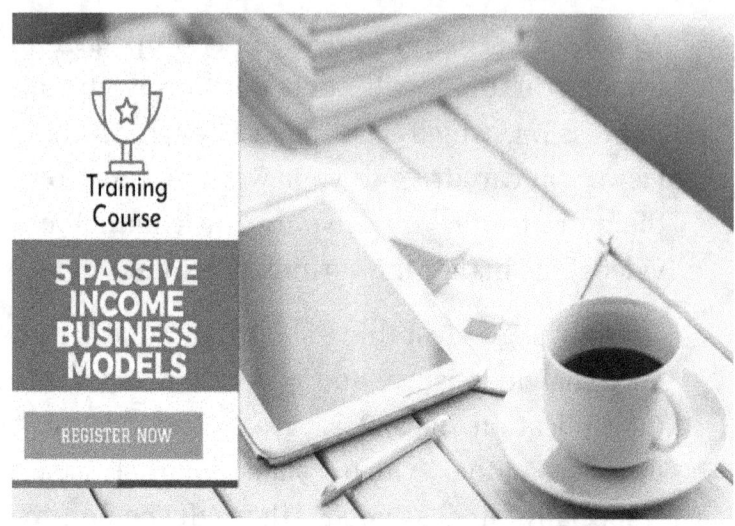

https://quintons-school.teachable.com/

6th Strategy: Ecommerce Site

One thing we know for sure is that how we shop has changed. Today, many of us would rather shop online. This has precipitated the rise of ecommerce moguls who are earning millions of dollars per month. Here, think along the lines of Amazon, Alibaba, eBay, Etsy, Baidu, and other similar ones.

You too can start such a business without having to give up your day job. Here is how:

Step 1: Decide What to Sell

The prospect of creating a successful ecommerce site hinges on having something to sell; without a product, getting started will not be easy. This pays credence to the importance of having a great product to sell.

The best way to go about deciding what to sell is to create something that solves a problem (solving a problem is central to online success) or take something in existence, make it better and then market it better. The second option is easier if you are not a creator.

When choosing a product, pay attention to niches you find familiar and are passionate about because selling something you are not familiar with means you will waste a lot of time trying to figure out how to connect with, or sell to the target audience. When you restrict yourself to a niche you are familiar with, you make this process much easier.Amazon is a great place to look for niche ideas for ecommerce sites.

The following resources should help you with finding the perfect products for your ecommerce store:

https://www.shopify.com

https://www.shopify.com

https://www.bigcommerce.com

https://www.ecomdash.com

Step 2: Source the Product

Those already making money in the ecommerce scene will willingly tell you that Alibaba is the best place to source for products. To use Alibaba, all you have to do is head to the site, type in the main keywords for the product you chose, and choose manufacturers who meet your specific criteria. As a rule, go with gold suppliers.

Step 3: Set up Your Store and Start Selling

Once you have a supplier for your product, the next step is to create your store. Here, you can create a store on sites such as Amazon, Etsy, eBay or Shopify, or create your own ecommerce website. Here, if you know nothing about ecommerce, you can recruit a capable web designer on sites such as Upwork.com or Freelancer.com and others.

After setting up your site, start uploading content descriptions for your merchandise and selling. To sell, however,

Step 4: Drive Traffic to Your Site

To drive traffic to you ecommerce site, you can use paid advertising (as long as the return on investment is ok), or seek organic traffic by performing SEO on the site content.

As an example, if you create a store than offers 5 products priced at $20, of which you 100 products per month per product, if the initial cost of creating and shipping the product is $10, it means in a month, your gross profit could be $5,000, give or take. This is without having to work tons of hours to generate the same.

Further Reading

https://ecommerce-platforms.com

http://www.huffingtonpost.com

https://www.shopify.com

https://www.oberlo.com

https://www.shopify.com

7th Strategy: Service Arbitrage Business

The other way you can generate a passive income is by selling other people's service, i.e. you act as a paid intermediary between those seeking services and those selling them. The best example of such sites is most freelancing websites such as Upwork.com, Fiverr.com, iWriter.com, Freelancer.com and the likes.

The idea behind this is relatively simple: find people looking to offer specific services online, services such as writing, find clients willing to pay for the same services at a rate higher than the one asked by the service provider, connect the two (preferably through a web portal) and pocket the difference.

Getting started on this business model is easy and very straightforward: all you need is to choose the service you want to arbitrage. This could be a service such as SEO analysis, book covers, social media management and marketing, etc. Once you have this core service in mind, start looking for service providers offering such services. You can find many of these on freelancing sites and then foster a relationship with them.

The next step is to search for clients looking for people seeking these services, offer to provide the services at a rate higher than what you shall offer the service provider and voila, you are in business. The greatest thing about this is that it does not require much time or much from you in terms of monetary investment.

For instance, if you decide to arbitrage "SEO analysis services," you can find a great service provider who is willing to offer amazing SEO services at $1,000 and on the other hand, a company that is willing to pay someone $1,500 for the same service. If you sell yourself as a great service provider for this company, and if the person you hire does an amazing job, you can earn $500 from being an intermediary.

The down side to this type of business is that it will take a substantial amount of time to create a convincing profile for the specific service you are offering. However, if you are good at this, which you can manage—creating trust and credibility—by creating an amazing portfolio site for the specific service you are arbitraging, you can be well on your way to earning thousands of dollars per week.

For instance, assume that it takes you about 6 months to create a great portfolio site for SEO analysis service and that on a weekly basis, 3 web owners reach out for your services (because you have already established yourself as an authority on the subject) paying $1500 each. If you outsource the same service to your capable service provider for $1,000, you can pocket the difference, which is $1,500 for the three clients. If this holds week-in-week-out, you can earn $4,500 with the potential to earn so much more as your business grows.

The most amazing thing about service arbitrage is that it is labor free: all you have to do is find service providers, find companies seeking the services offered by these service providers, offer the services and once the contract is yours, simply offer it to the service provider at a lesser fee. While it sounds fraudulent, there is nothing fraudulent about it just as there is nothing wrong about retail arbitrage.

Further reading

https://www.entrepreneurs-journey.com

https://www.warriorforum.com

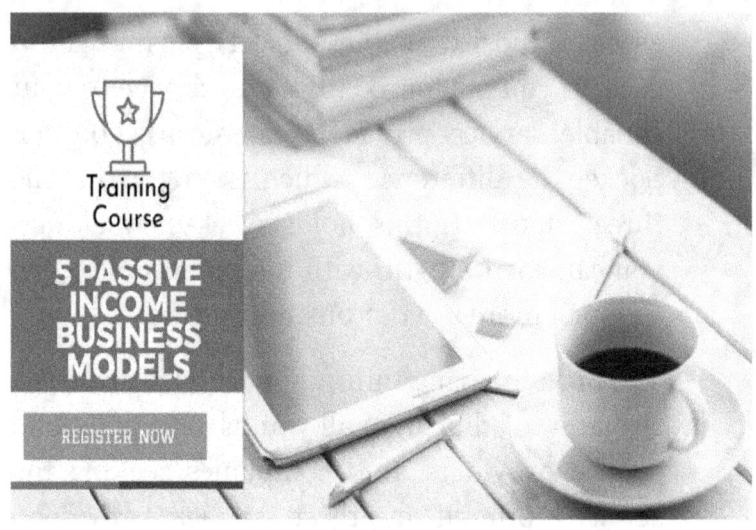

https://quintons-school.teachable.com/

Conclusion

We have come to the end of the book. Thank you for reading and congratulations for reading until the end.

This book has shown you 7 ways to create a passive income online. Implement these ways one after the other (setting up most requires less than 3 hours of work per day, which you can do before or after work), and in 6 months to 1 year, your business should be at a point where it earns you a steady income without the need for every day work.

When you get to that point, you shall be financially free and stable.

If you found the book valuable, can you recommend it to others? One way to do that is to post a review on Amazon.

Click here to leave a review for this book on Amazon!

Thank you and good luck!

DOWNLOAD YOUR FREE BONUS:

5 PASSIVE INCOME BUSINESS MODELS VIDEO COURSE

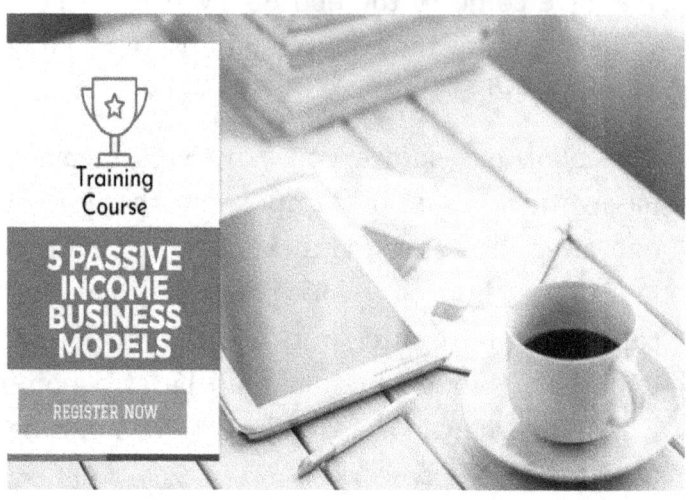

https://quintons-school.teachable.com/

I need your help......

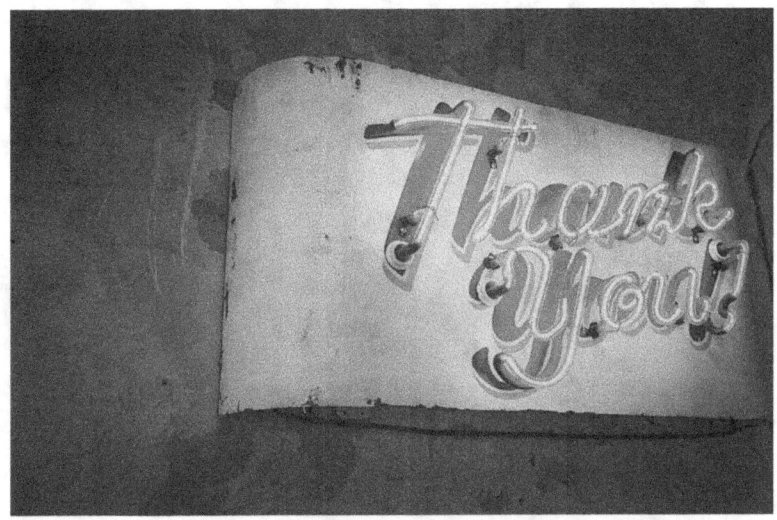

Thank you for purchasing and reading this book, I sincerely hope that you find value in the techniques and implement them into your life.

I created this book to help people start the journey of creating and building passive income streams. My goal is to let people know what options are available to them so that they can take advantage of them.

If you did find value in the book please take a minute to review the book and give your feedback as to what was good about and where it could improve.

This will help me in 2 ways:

1. It will help people decide if this book is worth buying.

2. Your feedback will help me make changes and improve the book.

www.ingramcontent.com/pod-product-compliance
Lightning Source LLC
Chambersburg PA
CBHW071514220526
45472CB00003B/1024